WAYS INTO GEOGRAPHY

Our Local Area

Louise Spilsbury

W

FRANKLIN WATTS
LONDON · SYDNEY

This edition 2012

First published in 2009 by
Franklin Watts
338 Euston Road
London NW1 3BH

Franklin Watts Australia
Level 17/207 Kent Street
Sydney NSW 2000

Series editor: Julia Bird
Art director: Jonathan Hair
Photography: Paul Bricknell (unless otherwise credited)
Design: Shobha Mucha
Artwork: John Alston
Consultant: Sam Woodhouse, Associate Consultant for
Geography and Citizenship, Somerset

A CIP catalogue record for this book is available
from the British Library.

Picture credits:
Alamy: cover: (r) Andrew Holt; 7: (t) Keith Morris; 15: (l) Robin Bath; p.24: Powered by Light/Alan
Spencer/Alamy; Corbis: 13: (l) Steve Chenn.istockphoto: 6: (b inset) David Hughes; 8: Jonathan Maddock; 10:
(tr) Owen Price, (tl) Steve Wignall, (bl) Steve Fawcett; 12: (t) istock; 13: (b) Ai-Lan Lee, 15: (br) Durden Images;
26: (b inset) Kateryna Govonuschenko. Shutterstock: cover: (l) David Hughes; 6: (t)Pres Panayatov, (t inset)
Rohit Seth; (b) David Hughes; 7: (b) Jacek Chabraszewski; 10: (bl) P Kruger; 12: (b) Ferenc Szelepcsenyi; 13: (t)
Kevin Eaves; 14: (t) Sean Nel, (b) Berto Paeli; 15: (t) Lynn Watson; 20: (r) Glen Gaffney; 24: (b) Tyler Olsen, 26:
(t) William Giakas, (b) Yuri Arcurs.

Every attempt has been made to clear
copyright. Should there be any inadvertent omission,
please apply to the publisher for rectification.

ISBN 978 1 4451 0952 7

Dewey Classification: 307

Printed in China

Franklin Watts is a division of Hachette Children's Books,
an Hachette UK company.
www.hachette.co.uk

Contents

Your local area

Your local area is the place around where you live. This is Ravi's local area. It is in a city.

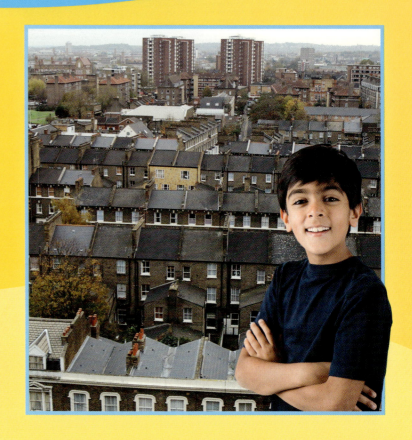

This is Josie's local area. It is in the countryside.

How are the two areas the same? How are they different?

Your local area includes the places you pass on the way to school. This includes places you need, like shops where you go to buy food.

There are also places where you have fun, like playgrounds.

What sort of places can you see in your local area?

What's an address?

An address tells people exactly where you live in your local area.

This is the number of the house or flat.

Sam Smith
5, York Street
Shelton
Hampshire
RG27 1AD

Next comes the name of the street or road.

Then you put the name of the village or town.

This is the name of the area or county where the village or town is.

The postcode is a set of letters and numbers that help the post office sort and deliver the post.

What is your address? Can you write it down?

Some of Ravi's class use their addresses to mark where they live on a street plan. A street plan shows all the streets in an area.

Who has the longest walk to school? Who has the shortest walk?

See if you can find where you live on a street plan of your local area.

Houses and homes

People live in different kinds of homes.

Flats

◁ Terraced houses

▽ Detached house

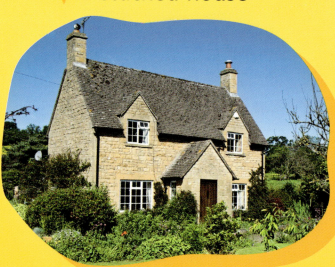

△ A caravan

What kind of home do you live in?
Have you ever stayed in a different kind of home?

Ravi's class makes a chart of the different homes the children live in.

	Type of home	With a garden	With a garage
Terraced	✔✔✔✔✔✔✔	✔✔✔✔✔✔✔	✔✔
Detached	✔✔✔	✔✔✔	✔✔✔
Semi-detached	✔✔✔✔✔✔	✔✔✔✔✔✔	✔✔✔✔✔✔
Flats	✔✔✔✔✔✔	✔	✔✔✔

What kind of home do most children in Ravi's class live in?
How many children have a garden at home?

Why do you think buildings look different?
Turn the page to find out.

Different buildings

Buildings look different because they have different purposes.

A fire station has big doors so the fire engines can get out quickly.

A cinema has no windows so that it is dark inside when films are showing.

Can you match these different buildings with the words in the box?

Barn
Hospital
Church

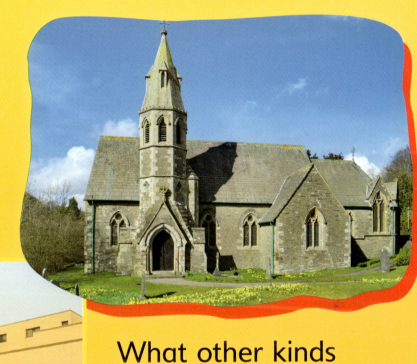

What other kinds of buildings can you name?

Emergency
Outpatient
Main Entrance

Places of work

Some buildings are places where people work.

In this office block, lots of people work at desks with computers.

In this factory, people use machines to make cars.

What jobs do people do in your local area?

Some people work in shops. You can often tell what shops sell by what is in their windows.

What kind of shops are these?

What different shops do you have in your local area?

Getting to school

Cerys walks to school, but her friends get there by car or take the bus.

Cerys decides to do a survey of the different ways children travel to school.

	Car	Bus	Bicycle	Walk
1	🚗	🚌	🚲	🧍
2	🚗	🚌	🚲	🧍
3	🚗	🚌	🚲	🧍
4	🚗	🚌	🚲	
5	🚗	🚌	🚲	
6	🚗	🚌		
7	🚗	🚌		
8	🚗			
9	🚗			
10	🚗			

She uses a computer to make a pictogram with the results of the survey.

Most children come to school by car. How many children cycle? How many walk?

How do the children in your class get to school?

On the way to school

Max sees a lot of different buildings on the way to school. He decides to draw his favourite building.

Describe what you see on the way to school. What smells and sounds do you notice?

Which part of your local area would you draw?

Sally makes a map of the route she takes to school. Symbols show where things are. Symbols are shapes or letters that represent real things.

A key explains the symbols.

Describe the route Sally takes to school.

Can you draw a map of your route to school?

Nice or nasty?

Cerys takes photos of the places she likes and dislikes in her local park.

I don't like the litter by this bench.

I like the flowers in this garden.

What parts of your local area do you like?
What parts do you dislike?

Cerys finds out where there is most litter in her local area.
Why is there litter in these places?

The Worst Litter

By the burger van

Near the sweet shop

In the park

Why Litter is There

People drop burger wrappers

People drop sweet wrappers and crisp packets

People sit here to eat lunch

How will Cerys solve the litter problem? Turn over to find out.

Make it better

Cerys asks the park manager to buy more bins for the park.

How should the new bins help to solve the litter problem?

The children in Cerys' class also make a poster to encourage people not to drop litter.

What would you put on a poster?
How could your local area be improved?

Changes

Local areas are always changing. Some changes improve the area. Some may spoil it.

People may build new homes in an area.

Sometimes, people have to cut down trees to make room for more homes.

These two maps show how Sam's local area has changed since his grandma was a child.

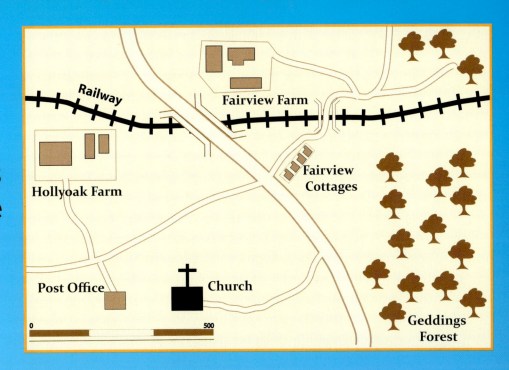

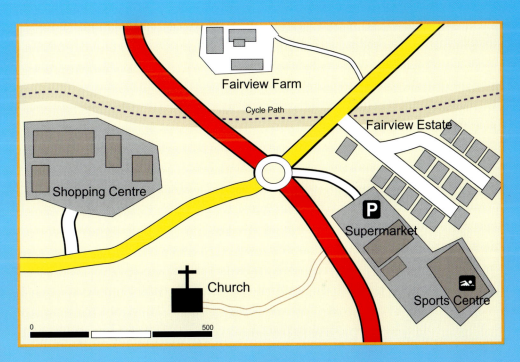

Sam likes the sports centre. His grandma wishes there was still a forest there to walk in.

What other changes can you see?

What was your local area like in the past? How has it changed?

Other areas

This is Hasan's local area. He lives in Morocco. Morocco is a hot country. The houses here are painted white to keep them cool.

This is Hannah's local area. She lives in Norway. Norway is a cold country. The houses here have sloping roofs so snow slides off them.

How are these buildings the same or different to buildings in your local area?

This map shows where Hannah and Hasan live.

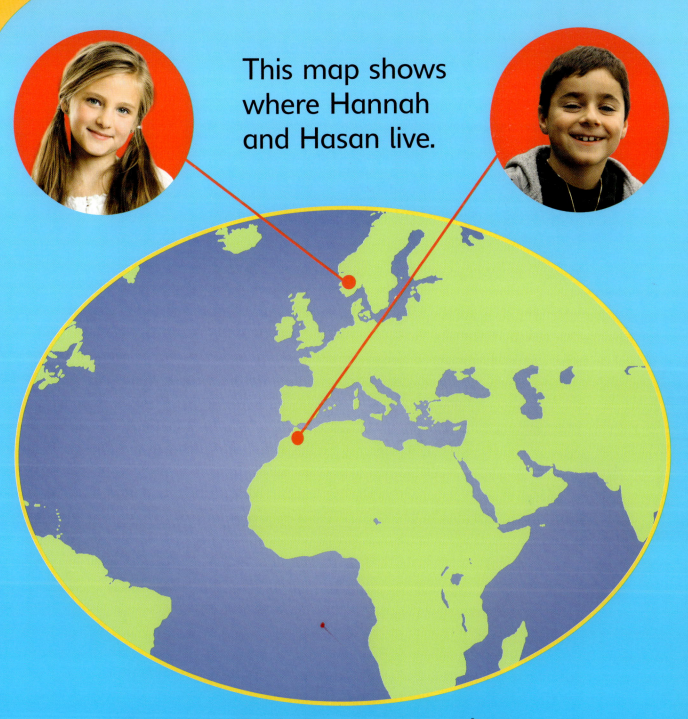

Can you find the country where you live on this map?
Is Hannah's or Hasan's country nearer to where you live?

Useful words

Address - an address tells people exactly where someone lives. It includes the number of their house, street name, village or town and country.

Factory - a building where workers use machines to make things.

Key - a key explains the symbols used on a map.

Local - the area that makes up your neighbourhood.

Map - a drawing of an area as if you were looking at it from above. There are different kinds of maps.

Pictogram - a chart or graph that uses pictures to show and compare information.

Purpose - what something is used for. The purpose of a fire station is to store fire engines.

Route - the way that you travel or plan to travel to get from one place to another.

Street plan - a street plan shows all the streets in an area.

Survey - to find out what a number of people think or do about a specific thing.

Symbol - shapes or letters that represent real things. A symbol for a wood might be a drawing of a tree, for example.

Some answers

Here are some answers to the questions we have asked in this book. Don't worry if you had different answers to ours; you may be right, too. Talk through your answers with other people and see if you can explain why they are right.

Page 6: Both areas have a road, shops and houses. But the village has a narrow street, few shops and fields around it, while a city street has a lot more traffic, high rise buildings and many shops.

Page 9: Mark has to walk the furthest to school and Annabel lives nearest.

Page 11: The chart shows that the most children in Ravi's class live in terraced houses and that 18 children have a garden at home.

Page 15: There is a florists that sells flowers, a hardware shop that sells equipment for the home, such as bins and kitchenware and a grocers that sells fruit and vegetables.

Page 17: The chart shows that 5 children cycle to school and that 3 children walk.

Page 19: To get to school, Sally turns left out of her house. She crosses the High Street and turns right. She walks past the post office and the church. She then turns left into North Street and walks until she reaches the school which is on the left-hand side of the street.

Page 22: When there are litter bins close by, people are more likely to use them.

Page 25: The railway line is no longer in use and is now a cycle track. There is no longer a post office near the church. Hollyoak Farm is gone and there is a large shopping centre in its place. Geddings Forest has been replaced by a supermarket and a sports centre. There are more homes in the area now: the cottages have been demolished and a large new housing estate called Fairview Estate has been built close by.

Index

About this book

Ways into Geography is designed to encourage children to think about the local and wider world in a geographical way. This title **Our Local Area** is a way in for children to study their local area, which is one of the two locality studies required at KS1.

By working through the book, they will also be learning the following **geographical skills**:
1. How to ask geographical questions (National Curriculum 1a)
2. How to observe and record (National Curriculum 1b).

Learning content

By using this book, children will also:
1. Consider changes in their own local area and the things they like or dislike about their local area and express their own views about places (National Curriculum 1c).
2. Look at pictures of homes and other buildings in places in the wider world and compare them directly to their own local area. What is the same and what is different? Can they explain why there are differences? Are they to do with weather, local building materials, and the different types of work in the two areas? This and work on earlier spreads will help them 'identify and describe what places are like' (National Curriculum 3a) and 'recognise how places compare with other places' (National Curriculum 3d).

Previous work and resources

It will help to have done some previous work with the children on using simple maps. On pages 8–9 it will help to have available a basic street map of the area around the school for children to look at. They could plot all kinds of features on this or maybe add photos linked by string with some of the places they use or go to. They could also use the street plan to help them draw the route they take to school, as suggested on pages 16–17. It might help the children's understanding of symbols and how and why they are used (so they are clear and can be understood by everyone, even if you cannot read or speak a different language) to look at common symbols in everyday use that they might see, such as signs on lavatory doors or the sign used by a lollipop person outside school? The last spread (26–27) can be used as an extension activity.